PEEPERS

PEEPERS

The Unsolicited Neighborhood Watch

D. D. MILES

Pittman Articles & More

By D. D. Miles

Dedications

To my husband the late, Demetriss Miles. and grandparents, James and Doris Pittman, and Elgertha Gosha, I dedicate this book to you. I wished you all were here to see its fulfillment, but Heaven needed some of their angels back. You will forever live through the pages of this book. Rest in Jesus my beloveds.

-Dee Dee

Psalm 8:3-9

Acknowledgments

First giving all honor and glory to God, I'd like to thank my mother, Janice Williams for her loving support. It's not every day that you have an avid reader, who so happens to be a retired Language Arts teacher, at your disposal. So if my subjects and verbs do not agree, or perhaps you come across some misspelled words, blame her. I'm just kidding, but thank you, mommy, for everything. You are priceless. To my dad, Larry Gosha who is my cheerleader and so supportive. I thank you, dad, for everything as well; your encouragement matters greatly. Thank you to my family and friends for your support as well. As you can see, I can't take full credit for any of this. I am so grateful to those who have come into my life to inspire and motivate me. To you, I say thank you as well.

To my Creative team: Reginald and Felicha Fisher, I thank you both for helping me to bring my visuals to life. I thank you especially, Felicha Fisher, for being a mighty force to reckon with. You are my mentor, sister, and friend. Thank you for all the love, countless prayers, and wisdom you've shared with me. **Editor**, Khalil Nasir, **Artist**,

Derrick Goudy, thank you both for everything!

To the Reader: I thank you for taking out the time to read this novella. I pray this

book will cause you to reminisce on days gone by and laugh greatly. **So let's get started, turn the page...**

3

Chapter 1

"**Ooowee Walt!** You ought to see 'em go. Necks rolling, fingers pointing, and tongues justa waggin' Look at 'em, just cussing up a storm," Birdie Abrams told her husband, who could have cared less. "Walt! Walt! Are you listening to me?" She asked, still peeping through the curtains.

"Yeah, I hear you, Birdie," he answered, still not caring. "Birdie, you had better come out of that window before someone throws a brick in here and smack you upside the head with it.

Back in my day, that's how we took care of nosey neighbors."

"Humph, I wish somebody would," she declared, rolling her eyes. "This is my window, in my house!" I can look out of it, and even go outside if I wanted to. They're the ones outside his mama's house acting a dang fool, and causing a scene. Look at 'em. It don't make no kind of sense for them two girls to be fussing over somebody who ain't worth two dead flies at a funeral.

Just a shame before the Master if you ask me."

"That's just it Birdie, don't nobody ever ask you," Walter Abrams mumbled under his breath.

Birdie gave Walter the hardest eye roll she could muster. What she didn't understand is how he could care so little about what was going on across the street. She felt it was her duty as a citizen to look out for her neighbors. *He'd* always been that way. If it didn't take place within his four walls, appeared in the newspaper, on that TV, down at the barbershop, or in Deacon meeting, he could care less. I betcha if you asked him who robbed Peter and then shot Paul, he could tell you that word for word. But something as simple as what was going on right now, across the street from his house, he wouldn't stop reading the paper long enough to come and see it. Go figure, she thought. "I still don't know why I should have to stop looking out of my window," she said, continuing to peep through the curtains. "We've been living on this street longer than those loud mouths out there have been alive, and I have a right to keep up with the activities on this street."

"And the next street, and the next street, and the street after that one," He said

"We all have to work together to keep our neighborhood safe, Walter."

"Um-hmm, and what part of spying on the neighbors is keeping the neighborhood safe, Birdie?" He asked, still looking at his paper.

"That's a matter of opinion, Walter. I'm just doing the neighborly thing since we don't have a neighborhood watch."

"Whatever you say, Dear." Walter knew not to waste any more of his precious time arguing with Birdie since she was going to do what she wanted to anyway, so why fuss?

"Anyway, Natalie would be devastated to know her son was out here carrying on like this. Outside of his poor mama's house too." "What a shame. And what makes this so crazy, he don't even live there. Now, why couldn't he have taken this mess to his neighborhood,?" Birdie asked.

"Because if he had, then you wouldn't have anybody to peep on," Her husband mumbled behind his paper.

"You are really trying my patience today, Walter Abrams. No, that's not it." She snapped back. "It's just he just knows better. Those people wouldn't dare put up with this type of foolishness in their up-scale neighborhood, so why bring it over here?"

Birdie was getting ready to give her husband more reasons why when she saw Alfreda Johnson, one of her nearest and dearest friends and fellow neighborhood watchwoman cutting across their yard.

Before Alfreda could make it to the porch good, Birdie flew out the front door just as fast as it would open. "Freda have a seat, out here honey, that way we won't miss a single thing."

"That's my whole purpose of coming over here. I'm trying to figure out what the commotion is all about, and that stupid hedge of mine was all in the way. See, on your porch you can see everything. Hey, Abrams." Alfreda spoke to Walter as she saw him sitting on the sofa.

Birdie's husband purposely ignored Alfreda as if she wasn't speaking to him. He couldn't stand her. Walter would never forgive Alfreda for causing him to lose his best friend. He also blamed her for creating tension in his marriage between him and his wife Birdie from time to time. No Sir, he would never forgive her. It was all her fault, and unless the good Lawd told him differently, he was not going to forgive her. Joseph "Bighead" Johnson was the best there was and the best there will ever be. Joe was like a brother to Walter. They grew up together in the Mobile Bay area until Joe decided to leave the paper mill. He'll never forget the letter he sent, encouraging him to move to Birmingham. At that time, Joe had landed a job at the US Steel plant and could get Walter a job there too. True enough, just as Joe promised, he did. Soon after that, he had met the prettiest young thing he had ever seen. There she was working in a local café, serving up hot sandwiches and coffee. Then when he took his first seat in Mt Zion Baptist Church, he looked up in the choir stand, the sweetest pair of eyes were staring back at him, their gazes locked, and she became his sweet Birdie from that day forward.

After he and his young bride were married, they looked all over for a place. It just so happened, the house they found was right next door to Joe and Alfreda. During that time, Walter felt like life couldn't get any better for them; two boys out of Mobile living and working side by side. He was able to feed his family of four, and Birdie didn't have to work at the café anymore, they were doing good. All she had to do was make a good home for him and raise their children. After a while, he had begun to notice Joe taking on extra hours, not spending as much time at home, or with anyone else, for that matter. The man was working his fingers to the bone. Come to find out, it was just to buy 'Freda' as he called her, the finer things in life. Every time he turned around, Joe was buying this and that. Joe had pretty much ran himself into the ground. One day at work, he collapsed and was admitted into the hospital.

The doctor had given him a hard warning to stop working so much, because it wasn't good for his heart. Considering the advice of the doctor, Joe slowed up and started cutting back, but Alfreda was having no parts of that. She wanted to be able to show off her beautiful big house and fancy furniture. It didn't make sense to Walter then, and it still doesn't now. Alfreda was a teacher, and although they didn't make a lot of money, she didn't have to have all those things either. To him, they were doing better than alright; shoot, they had it better than most families did. These were the things they talked about being as young boys growing up. They saw their fathers provide and they wanted to be able to do the same for their own.

Joe had had enough one day. He told Alfreda, "You won't be satisfied until I kill myself out here working like a driven horse. Is that what you want for me, to die!!!?" Joe had come to the realization Alfreda was all about the material things at his expense. She only cared about the things he did for her, nothing for him personally. Walter re-called those times when she tried to drag Joe's innocent name through the mud, and even tried to convince his wife that he, himself, had put Joe up to divorcing her. Walter was saddened to learn his friend's life ended up like this. Never in a million years would he imagine Joe giving up on what he once loved. But Joe made all those decisions for him-self and left Birmingham a broken man. That witch made sure his old friend had nothing left to his name. Walter was devastated by the pain his best friend suffered and felt helpless because it was nothing he could do to help him.

Years had passed by when Joe reached out to his old friend Walter. He was surprised to hear Joe had remarried, and that he was happier now than he had ever been. Walter was very happy for him but missed him dearly. Every year the two, along with their wives, would find a nice trip to go on. This year they planned to go on a cruise to Mexico, but somehow Alfreda had come up with the brilliant idea to include herself on their trip after reading their brochure. Walter strongly suggested to her that unless she thought she could drink the Gulf of Mexico, to pass on going on that ship with them. She and Joe may have allowed bygones to be bygones, but he and Alfreda hadn't.

"**WALTER!** I know you heard Alfreda speaking to you. Sitting there like you ain't heard nobody say nothing, Birdie fussed.

Walter slowly came out of his thoughts of Joe, pulled down the corner of his paper, just enough to hide the smile on his face. He didn't want Alfreda to think his genuine smile had anything to do with her. All he had for her was an acknowledgment, "Alfreda." He had no intention of saying anything else, but since Birdie insisted, he provided the driest pleasantry he could muster.

He didn't want to know how she was feeling, if all was well, if she was having a great day -- nothing. After he acknowledged her mere presence, he quickly pulled up the corner of his paper, and continued to read about America's financial crisis, wondering what they were going to do about it.

"Look over him, honey." Birdie told Alfreda as she sat next to her. "If his head ain't in them doggone sports, it's in them newspapers," She said apologetically to her friend.

"That's alright. It's no need of him to be so rude to me 'cause I know I hadn't done one single thing to him, I'll just let God handle him. What happened between Joe and me took place many years ago. He and I made amends, raised our children, got on with our lives, and Walter just needs to do the same. It makes little to no sense to harbor ill will like that towards people.

That's the very thing Pastor preached about last Sunday. He told us to get out of our feelings.

Holding grudges toward people just ain't right, and God isn't pleased. "You better know that Abrams!" Alfreda shouted.

Birdie listened to her friend's gripe about Walter's dislike for her, but she also knew her loving husband too. He was never going to get over Joe's leaving, and no matter how much she recited what Pastor said, Walter had a made-up mind of his own. That was one losing battle that she could no longer fight.

She was just about to apologize again for Walter's behavior when the argument across the street got louder. Fooling around with her husband and Freda, she was about to miss something good.

"Dee, all I want to know is why this trick all up in your parents' house?" Moet demanded to know.

"First of all, baby, I ain't no trick, don't get me confused with you, and second of all, it ain't none of yo business what me and my man doing up in my soon to be in-law's house," She said, pointing her finger in Moet's face.

"Quinisha!" Darius yelled. Hood chicks, he thought, shaking his head. Why do they have to be so freakin' dramatic?

"What she talkin' bout, Darius? What does she mean, her man, soon-to-be? I don't have time to be playing games with y'all."

"Make time, 'cause you heard right. He and I made it official last night. Mmm, hmm, we sure did." She said, trying to lock arms with Darius. "So you can move on with your pitiful little life," Quinisha said, taunting her and waving her hand Moet's way.

Darius removed his arm and stood in between the two women in hopes of preventing the physical altercation that was surely about to pop off. These two have a history that fuels back from high school. If anything, all Quinisha was doing was reigniting the feud. Why she would even test Moet, only God knows. She should know by now and by experience that it will not turn out well for her.

"Is that true, Darius? Is this what you are doing now?" Moet asked with what appeared to be pain in her eyes, and tears rolling down her face. This was the final straw for her. Moet thought they were working on something special, but all he had done was lie to her. She was so sick of his mind games and was ready to pick up the closest thing next to her. She didn't know if she should hit him with that empty beer bottle she just spotted for lying or hit that piece of nothing standing on the other side of him. Quinisha really wasn't worth it.

She always allowed her mouth to write checks that she knew her butt couldn't cash. Of all the women he could've hooked up with, why her? Compared to herself, Quinisha was nothing, a hood rat looking for her next meal ticket. If it weren't for her cousin Carmen, Darius would've made yet another fool out of her, but not this time, she thought. This time, she was going to make sure it would be his last.

"Look, man, y'all need to stop it. Y'all got all the neighbors coming out of their houses,"

Darius told them, looking around at all the people watching. "This ain't no show!" He yelled out at the neighbors angrily.

Birdie and Alfreda, who had front-row seats, looked at each other.

"I know he ain't talking to us," Alfreda said to Birdie.

"Uh-uh, I know that's right."

"Evidently, it is a show! You too stupid to take 'em both in the house where prying eyes can't see!" Birdie yelled back across the street.

All the neighbors who were standing outside were laughing at him, and nothing at all was funny about this. He didn't want to be involved in another shouting match, especially with those two across the street. They were able to get into contact with his folks at a moment's notice, and he didn't need his dad down his throat about this bull. Especially since it wasn't what Moet thought it was, and what Quinisha was trying to make it out to be.

What he wanted was for both of the women to leave, but neither was going to budge an inch. He had told Moet a thousand times to stop popping up at his parent's house unannounced.

Now he has to play referee by standing in between two grown women who were ready to thump at a moment's notice. He didn't need this drama in his life, but Ms. Birdie did have a point.

"Look! Let's take this into the house. But I'm warning y'all, if anything in my parent's house gets broken, I'm calling the cops, and having both of y'all arrested." As commanded, Moet led the way while Darius remained in the middle.

"Looks like the shows over, Birdie."

"Yeah, I see. I guess I'll go in and start on dinner." Birdie said.

"What happened, anyway?" Alfreda asked.

"Well, that short one spent the night last night, I believe," Birdie told her.

"Knowing her, she probably did. You know she's always been hotter than a firecracker. I heard somebody say that she was one of those exotic dancers."

"Exotic dancer? What kind of dancing is that?"

"The kind that you take all your clothes off for."

"You mean a stripper, Alfreda?"

"Yes, a stripper."

"Just say stripper, honey. I don't know nothing about them fancy titles."

"Well, that's what I heard about her. I thought I had seen that car parked in their driveway this morning."

"Un-huh, you did. Well, about ten minutes ago, the blond one came flying around that corner like a banshee out of hell. She pulled up on them, as the children say."

"Makes me wonder if her cousin, what's her name, had anything to do with this, 'cause you know that child stay to herself. She has a beauty shop doing well for herself. She don't have time for this mess," Alfreda told her.

"Girl, if you know like I do, she did, messy self. I saw her walking that itty-bitty dog past the house this morning. Just like you, she noticed that the car was there too. She couldn't dial those numbers on that phone fast enough."

"Lawd out of all seventy-two years of my life, I've never seen folks act a fool like that."

"Hmph, you should've met me back in my teen days, 'cause baby I was a something else." "Birdie, what you talkin' bout?" Alfreda asked with a slight giggle. She had known Birdie Abrams for quite some time and had heard a tale or two. It wasn't hard to believe Birdie was a pistol back then, because she's just as fiery now.

"Baby, if that were me out here when I was in my late teens' and early twenties, and she was up in my face talking about her and my man, it wouldn't have been anything left to say. She would've been cut five ways before she had realized what happened to her."

"Birdie!"

"What! Baby, I thank God for Jesus. 'Cause since I've been saved, I'm not like that anymore. But I still wouldn't have been the one standing in the middle of the street, looking like no fool now. Personally, I think they should've jumped him."

"Birdie, are you really sitting here condoning violence?"

"No, all I'm saying is they should've went upside his head. Them girls didn't know he had been cheating on one with the other one. You better know one of them meant business, baby. Did you see how that girl with the blond hair had her fist balled up? She was about to give a whole new meaning to butt whuppin. That other girl you said was a stripper was about to get it, baby."

"Still, I don't think they should be fighting, especially over no man."

"Say what you want, I never had to worry about them women down there at that plant nor the church, because you better believe they all knew about Birdie Watson, baby. She didn't play about hers."

"Birdie, I just think they both need to leave him alone."

"You know, just like I do that ain't gon' happen."

"But still Birdie those girls can do better. They don't need this mess in their lives."

"What those girls need to do is whoop...his...butt, that'll teach him to cheat."

"Why do you dislike him so much?"

"Cause he thinks he's God's gift to women, even as a little boy he did. Almost had my Kenya in his nasty little clutches, calling himself liking her, but I busted that thang up before it could even get started."

"Girl, no! When did all this happen?" She asked.

"Oh yes, I did too." Birdie said. "I believe it happened during the summer when they all had graduated from high school. Well, let me say that's when I began to notice some things. I remembered it like it was yesterday. Kenya was down here visiting for the summer when he tried to be slick. I saw her fast tail out here one day justa cheesing, honey. I don't know what he was telling her, but she liked it. I had to call that little heffa's name at least five times before she finally heard me, but the next time I saw him, I told him to stay his little horny you know what away from my granddaughter."

"I'm surprised Kenya would take a liking to someone like that."

"Honey, please, folks like what they like, but if she could've seen what I saw, she wouldn't have talked to him in the first place."

"I'll give this to her, at least she knows what to attract. Darius is a good-looking young fella with a great job, and no kids. She could've done worse. I'm just saying, in my book, that's a catch for anybody. But you know he takes those looks after his mother's side of the family. You remember Johnathan Rogers, don't you?" Alfreda asked Birdie. "Those Rogers men sure did have it going on back in the day. I think it was about seven of them."

"Oh yeah, I remember seeing him and his wife Grace all the time over there at the house."

"Those brothers knew they could turn some heads. My twin sister Alberta once dated one of them, but it didn't last long. Talk about a skirt chaser, ooh girl! It was awful."

"When we moved here in fifty-two, they were making plans to build a new home in Adamsville. I remember when they gave Darius' mother their house when she graduated from college, soon after that, she married Douglas, and then had him."

"That's right; they sure did give her that house. That child looks just like his granddaddy, from the cashew brown skin, wavy black hair, to those hazel colored eyes. He's even tall like him. Grace, God rest her soul, had to put her foot down many a day. Women went crazy over her husband, and then he owned a convenience store, too. Can you imagine the foot traffic of women coming in and out of that store? No shame whatsoever, for whatever reason they could find. I know some women to this day whose husband's hard-earned money built their second home out there in Adamsville."

"Alfreda, you ought to stop."

"I ain't lying, Birdie. I wish Louise was at home, she'd tell you the same thing. Those women were in and out of that store like it was a terminal at the airport."

"Well, I'm glad Kenya lives in DC. They haven't seen each other in years."

"How's she doing anyway?"

"She's fine. She called us earlier today to tell us she'll be flying in tomorrow. I can't wait to see my baby. We haven't seen her in a while."

"It's so good how she finds time to visit her grandparents. Do you all have big plans?" Alfreda asked.

"Not really. Kenya called and..."

Is all Birdie could say, because the action had just picked back up across the street. Both girls had just stormed out of the house, one behind the other.

"So y'all think y'all can just destroy my parent's sixty-flat-inch flat screen, and not have to pay for the damages?"

"You deserve more than that, butthole," Qunisha said, walking to her car.

"She's right, you do!" Moet yelled.

Moet found the closest brick to her and threw it at the windshield of Darius's brand new custom Nissan 370Z as hard as she could, causing it to shatter.

"**Noooooooooo!**" Darius screamed.

Birdie and Alfreda stood to their feet. They didn't know if they were going to witness a possible murder or what, but what they did know was that Darius was .38 hot and was about to go ballistic. It was a good thing that they were sitting outside, because the other girl had driven off, and if they weren't there, only God knows what would have happened next. The ladies couldn't believe what they were witnessing. This girl had the nerve to stand there, daring him to do something about it.

"She better get her stupid butt in that car and leave before something bad happens to her." Birdie said, whispering to Alfreda.

"You got that right. Little girl, this ain't the time to stand toe to toe."

Darius knew if he hit her, he would go to jail automatically. He wanted to smack that smirk right off her face. Her brazenness was asking him to hit her. His tightly clenched teeth and fist were starting to hurt. It was all he could do to take out his cell to call the police, instead of launching at her neck as his thoughts were begging him. He was going to let it go with the television and replace it with something better for his parents, but to smash the windshield on his brand new car was something else. Thank God it wasn't the truck.

"I would like to file a police report for property damage, and to request a restraining order," He told the operator, turning around to go back into his house. Leaving Moet standing there ranting, **"Yeah, that's right, call the police, punk!"** she yelled at him.

Less than ten minutes later, the police had arrived and were asking Darius all kinds of questions and taking the report. Moet hadn't moved an inch, and Birdie and Alfreda were still standing on the front porch, shocked and confused. They didn't know whether they should go over to see if the girl was all right, if she was too upset to drive, or what. They've seen many bricks thrown in their days, but never had anyone stayed behind, especially after the police were called.

They watched as the police asked her a series of questions and informed her that she had to leave the victim's home. That's when Moet lost it.

"I'm the victim. He's not! Did he tell y'all what he did to me!?"

"Yes ma'am, he did, but you can't stay here, you must leave. You're lucky he decided not to press charges, Ms. Perkins. Please take our advice and leave the premises now."

"That's it? I leave, and there's nothing else?" She said, walking back and forth, looking at him.

"Ms. Perkins, please don't make this harder than it has to be. I understand that you are upset with Mr. Avery, and don't get us wrong, we understand, but you can't stay here."

"Okay, Officer, I'll leave as soon as you make him apologize for being so foul."

"I'm sorry, ma'am, but I can't make him apologize, either."

"Well, what can you do then, because... You know what? Forget it!" She said out of frustration. "Don't worry about it. Y'all can't help me anyway." She told the police officer and slammed her car door, and drove off talking to someone on her cell phone.

"You know no good will come of this. It's a wonder they didn't arrest her." Birdie said to Alfreda.

"You ain't kidding. Did you see the look she gave Darius before she left?"

"Un-huh, but what I don't understand is why she didn't leave."

"Unlike the other girl, when she saw that brick flying, she took off."

"I know that's right." They laughed. "But Alfreda, I got a bad feeling about this one."

"Me too, Birdie, but we'll have to wait and see what'll happen next."

Chapter 2

"Qunisha, we have nothing else to talk about! Stop calling me with this BS. You lied on me, and I helped you out last night! You know nothing is going on between us. Why would you lie like that, and on me of all people. I'm telling you, girl, the games you play are going to get someone killed one day. Messing around with you and your lies, I have a broken television and a cracked car windshield. Man, I don't want to hear your apologies, if you aren't talking about coughing up the dough for my TV, we have nothing else left to discuss." Darius didn't bother to say good-bye before hanging up. He had heard enough from her, and besides, there was a knock at the front door.

"Man I hate these...ugh!" Darius yelled out loud after seeing his friend.

"Man, D, what in tha world, dawg?" Jay asked him, walking into the house.

Darius sat next to Jay on the sofa, still reeling over yesterday's events. All last night he had been trying to figure out where it all went wrong, and being thankful it hadn't happened at his house. "Dude, you don't even know the half, man," He finally responded.

"Wanna bet." Jay chuckled. "And we both know how." "Carmen!" They said in unison.

"Man, Carmen talks too much. This is all her fault too. I just want you to know that. Had she kept her nose out of my business, Moet wouldn't have known Quinisha's car was even over here." He said, annoyed.

"Don't go blaming my girl 'cause you wanted to be a player," Jay said, laughing. "You think this is funny? Whatever man, I was not being a player. Quinisha was at the house yesterday because I drove her car to my parents the night before, but your girl, as usual in my business, got things all wrong, again."

"Partner, make me understand it then, because from what I hear you're engaged to Quin.

Quin, dawg?"

"You know good, and well that's not true. When have you ever known me to be that desperate?"

"Dude, I hear wild stuff all the time. You're engaged to one, and sleeping with both is the word on the street."

"The streets are lying, or should I say, Carmen. I'm not sleeping with either one of them. The other night, I was invited by a coworker to attend a birthday party, not knowing Quinisha would be there. Dawg, she was so drunk at this party that any man could have taken her home. Being that she is one of the homegirls, I looked out for her. I convinced her to give me the keys to her car. After I had them, I called her an Uber, had one of my friends tail me here in my car, and I dropped hers off. It's a good thing that his lady friend was so understanding, 'cause I would've had to call and wake your butt up to come get me."

"Man..."

"Yeah, so when Quinisha came to pick her car up the next day, all hell broke loose. Like I said, it's all Carmen's fault, had she just minded her business, none of this would have ever happened. But then again, she's got your nose so wide open, you'd believe just about anything she tells you. Me, being engaged to Quin, man, please. Who do you take me for?"

"Keeping it real, man, I know we've been best friends since we were kids, and I think I

know you better than anyone, but seriously, I thought you might have gotten caught up this time, homie."

"Nope, I hadn't done anything wrong. You need to talk to your girl, though. She needs to learn how to stay out of my business, man, like for real." He said, aggravated.

"Did you think for a moment, she wasn't going to tell Mo, you had some other chick at the house? C'mon man, you know her better than that."

"Whatever man, she had no reason to do that at all. Here are the real facts, I don't date either one of them. Besides, if you don't know what you're talking about, you should keep your mouth closed. She was wrong for giving Mo any information about something she knew nothing about, cousins or not. Now I'm the one who has to replace my parent's broken TV and a busted windshield. Are you going to pay for it for her, since she's so right to you?" Darius asked before taking another swig of his beer.

"No! She didn't tell Moet to wreck the place. That's all on them."

"That's what I thought. It's Carmen's fault. Moet and I are just friends, nothing more. Why she felt the need to report the activities going on at my parent's home is beyond me."

"That's not how I hear it. Man, they talk like y'all kicking it."

"You're hearing it from me now, and I'm telling you, to your face, nothing is going on between us. Yes, Moet is interested in me. Yes, I know this, but I can't help that. We're friends.

Correction, *was*."

"I hear you, man. Other than blaming my baby for this mess, what's up for tonight?" "Dude, you can't be serious. Did you not just pass by my covered up car, and do you not see my folk's TV right here? I ain't about to do nothin'. This situation has messed my whole weekend up."

"You know Big Mike is having that get together later on. You might want to fall through.

It'll help you get your mind off some of this craziness."

"Man, am I talking to myself? Dude, I'm not feeling any of that today. The only thing on my mind is calling a glass repair company for an estimate, and going outside to take pictures of the damage done to my car for the insurance company."

"I still can't believe she threw a brick into your windshield. They said she was crazy yo; I just didn't believe them until now."

"Man, whatever. Crazy or not, I want my windshield replaced and to be reimbursed for my parent's television. I'm not trying to hear 'wait until payday, I don't have it, or can we work something out?' None of it! I want my money. It meant nothing to her to bust my window, and it'll mean nothing to me to slap a lien against her property, if she don't pay," He said, grabbing up his phone.

Chapter 3

Darius and Jay were outside, removing the tarp off of his car when the Abrams' pulled into their driveway. He stared hard across the street in disbelief at the one he hadn't seen since they were teenagers. He'd never forgotten her. Kenya was the one girl that got away.

"Hey man, who is that, she thicker than a Snicker?" Jay asked.

Annoyed by the comment, he replied, "That's Kenya." She's the Abrams' granddaughter." He said as they continued watching her. "I haven't seen her since the summer we all graduated from high school."

"I know you didn't let that pass by and not try to holler at her."

"It wasn't up to me back then, dawg." He said, nodding his head at Mrs. Abrams, who was currently mean mugging them. Then he remembered her warning, "You may have these other little girls running behind you, but my baby won't be one of them. Don't look at her, don't talk to her, and you bet' not even think about her. Do you understand me, little mannish boy?" All he could say back then was yes ma'am, and by the way she was looking at him right now, she still meant business.

Mr. Abrams spoke to them as he was gathering Kenya's luggage together. The guys spoke to everyone. Darius could tell that Kenya may have recognized him, but that lil' old busy body known as her grandmother had pulled her into the house before he could address her. By the looks of her luggage, she may be here for a while, Darius thought. He wouldn't mind catching up with his old friend. She was so different from any girl he had ever met. Kenya was both smart and beautiful. She was the type not to let her looks go to her head like most women he knew, and because of her smarts, he knew she would going places in life.

After the threat from her grandmother, he knew he couldn't see her like he wanted, so he waited until they were hanging out with their mutual friends to spend time with her. During those occasions, they would laugh and talk and just have fun. She was a good girl, and he appreciated her friendship, but summer came to an end, and she moved to D.C. for school. He often thought about her and wondered whatever became of the sweet girl he once knew. It wasn't often that he got a chance to ask Mr. Abrams about her, and he knew better than to ask Mrs. Abrams anything.

To see her today gave him hope of getting all of those wonders fulfilled.

Darius noticed Mr. Abrams was still unloading luggage. He told Jay he'd be right back as he walked across the street to help.

"Hey, Mr. Abrams, it looks like you have your hands full. Would you like some help with those?"

"Son, yes I do. This gal has come down here with so much luggage, til' I asked her if she was running away. All of these suitcases for a week; it just don't make no sense. When we saw her at the airport, I asked my wife if she had planned on staying for a month. I told her then all she needed to pack was two pair of pants, three shirts, socks, a pair of shoes, a bra, and some draws. All of that I named could fit in one suitcase. Not her, she has three suitcases and a carryon. Son, you know this don't make no sense. Women! I'm too old to be hauling all this mess up and down them stairs. I tell you what, she better hope you somewhere around when she leaves,

'cause I ain't able to keep hauling all this mess around town." He said, still ranting.

By this time, Darius was so engulfed in laughter that he hadn't noticed Kenya standing next to him.

"Excuse me," he said, finally acknowledging her. "I don't know if you remember me, but-"

"Darius, of course I remember you." She said, giggling and hugging him. "It's been a long time."

What a beautiful smile, he thought. "Oh yeah, it has been. I came over to help your grandfather with the luggage."

"Thanks. I can take it from here. I wouldn't want to keep you from your company." She said, looking over at Jay. Mr. Abrams left them standing there to talk, leaving one suitcase behind.

"Oh, that's my boy, Jason. You might remember him too."

"He looks vaguely familiar. Wait, was he the kid that wore those thick eyeglasses and was allergic to everything?"

"Yep, that's Jay, all right," Darius said, laughing. "Corrective eye surgery, a lot of allergy shots, and there he is. Enough about him, though. How have you been? I haven't seen you in years. The last time I saw you, you'd broken my heart and left me to pick up the pieces." He said, pretending to wipe away the invisible tears.

"I did not. You were the one who promised to stay in touch. When I came back to visit, you had gone off to college. I heard through the grapevine that you had become the big man on campus."

"Football and fraternity stuff, but you know I would nev-" He said, being interrupted.

"Kenya, I need to talk to you about something!" Mrs. Abrams yelled out the door. "Okay, Granny, I'll be right there in just a sec," She replied. "I'm sorry, you were saying?"

"No, I'm sorry. I know you just got here, and I don't mean to keep you from your family. Do you think we-" Interrupted again. This time irritation was showing on his face. Today was not Mrs. Abrams's day to test his patience.

"Now, Kenya!" She insisted.

"Just a minute and I'll be right there," She told her grandmother, feeling annoyed. "Please continue before she cuts you off again."

"Do you mind if we went somewhere to just catch up?" He asked her.

"Sure, I'd like that. Here's my card. Call me a little later, and we can go over the details." He took her card, placed it in his pocket, and picked up her last suitcase.

He felt piercing eyes on him, and became face to face with the one owning them. He never noticed how much Kenya looked like her grandmother; beauty ran deep in their family. To be fair-skinned, Mrs. Abrams aged gracefully, she didn't have a flaw anywhere, but that icy stare of hers sent chills down his spine. Darius broke the silence by speaking to Mrs. Abrams. Ignoring his pleasantries, she snatched the suitcase out of his hands and walked into the house, slamming the wooden door behind her. "I'm afraid I'm not one of her favorite people," Darius told Kenya.

In complete shock, she apologized for her grandmother's behavior, "I've never seen her behave in such a way," Kenya said, frowning.

"Look, no worries," he said, grabbing her hand. "I will talk to you later, and we can pick up where we left off, okay?" He said, smiling.

In return she gave him a glowing smile and said, "Okay."

Regretfully he released her hand and prepared to watch her leave his sight.

"Do you need any more help?" He asked.

"No, everything's in the house now. I guess I'll be talking to you later," She said, smiling.

"Oh no, you won't, either!" Birdie said as she flung open the door.

"Grandmother!"

"Birdie!"

"What! Stop calling my name. And you," she said, pointing her boney finger at her granddaughter, **"Bring yourself into this house, right now!"** Birdie demanded.

Kenya apologized once again to Darius before going into the house. She was so embarrassed by her grandmother's behavior. He tried telling Kenya, she had nothing to apologize for, but she insisted. She didn't understand what had gotten into her grandmother but, she promised, she would definitely get down to the bottom of it.

Chapter 4

"Granny, what's wrong? You're yelling out the house at me like I was about to be eaten alive or something."

"Plain and simple, Baby girl, your grandmother's cheese done slide clean off of her cracker," Her grandfather said. "She's just crazy. I think it's them hair rollers she's been sleeping on all these years."

"What? What does that mean, Papa?" Kenya asked, laughing.

"In short, he's trying to call me crazy, but I need to remind him they don't let crazy people cook. And if he plan on eating ever again, he better take that comment back."

"Tell her, Honeybee. I don't have to take anything back. You'll cook for me, won't you, Buttercup?" He asked his granddaughter.

"Always, Papa." She smiled. "But, you two won't be involving me in your drama."

"Ain't nobody cookin' up in my kitchen, buddy." Birdie told her husband.

"That's fine. I have plenty of restaurants to eat at."

"That's fine, too; make sure it's one that can take care of all your needs, and I do mean all of your n-e-e-d-s, because my hair rollers might be too tight."

"Okay, that's it! No more of this, please. Delicate ears over here," Kenya said, laughing and covering her ears.

"Don't mind us, chile, but I do have something to talk to you about." "Oh, boy, here we go," Walter said, turning his news on and the volume up.

"Walter, must you turn the volume up so loud?" She asked him.

"Un-huh, don't nobody want to hear that foolishness you about to talk about."

"What foolishness? It's the truth!" She exclaimed

"What's the truth, Granny?"

"Well, girl, let me tell ya. Don't fool with that boy 'cross the street. Just yesterday, he had two women over there fussing and cussing over him, plus one of them bust the window out of his car."

Kenya started to laugh. "You mean like the song?"

"What song?" Birdie was completely confused.

"Never mind, Granny. As you were saying."

"She don't know what you talking about, baby. She ain't as hip as I am." Her grandfather claimed.

"Since we got cable, he thinks he knows every darn thing. Don't tell me nothing about them idiotic shows he watches on that TV. I, myself, watch the real world by sitting on that front porch. That's why I can say, don't fool with that boy across the street."

"There's no harm in having friends, Granny." She said that hoping she wasn't giving herself away. She melted on the inside when she saw Darius again. As a young girl, she thought he was so cute, but oh my God, time has been good to him. He is fine fine, and she couldn't wait for him to call. She did, however, have some apprehension. Not because of anything her Granny had said, but because she had drama to contend with of her own. She remembered her time with Darius being good, but there was a time he did act as if she hadn't existed, and she never knew why.

"Well, Baby girl, I don't want you to get caught up in no mess," her grandmother cautioned.

"Thanks for looking out gran, but I believe I can handle it; if not, I'll have my big bad grandpa to go over there and beat him up."

"Hmph, he ain't gone leave that chair for nothing in this world; besides, he likes that boy.

Instead of beating him up, he'd be over there laughing and talking with him like he always does.

That's all right; forget him. I'll handle it myself. You don't need your grandpa, use me."

"**No, you will not!** Birdie, stay out of her business and leave that boy alone." Her husband told her.

"**I will not!** He's not going to mess up her life with those lies he's been telling."

"You don't know that to be true, Birdie. But you will stay out of it, and that's final," Walter commanded.

Is that all? Kenya thought. She just knew this was going to be an argument that would go on forever. Her grandmother was very over-protective of her grandchildren. Always has been. But to interfere in their personal affairs has never happened before, even as adults.

Kenya, however, was nobody's fool. She had planned to ask Darius about his recent events, and although they were old childhood friends, it wasn't necessary to be caught up in the crossfire of any relationship drama.

Chapter 5

As Kenya walked into her old bedroom, she felt nostalgic. This place was where she had spent countless weekends, holidays, and summers. Her grandparents allowed her to decorate this room any way she wanted. She still had the stuffed teddy bears on the bed that her grandfather won for her at the County Fair. She stood by her bay window, remembering how she used to watch Darius and his friends play football, and how the girls would parade up and down the sidewalk to get their attention. She remembered Ms. Alfreda's granddaughter, Pepper, and a few other girls, being their so-called cheerleaders. Cayenne, as her Granny often referred to Pepper, had the biggest crush on Darius at one time, but that was short-lived when Ed moved into the neighborhood.

During the summer of their graduating year of high school, Ed had enlisted in the Navy, and before leaving, he and Pepper wed. Kenya served as one of her bridesmaids. She believed it was then that Darius started to take a liking to her. Most girls would have been flattered, but not

Kenya. By this time, he was riding around in his dad's Camaro, and could just about have any girl he wanted. At eighteen, the boy was fly and flashy. He had it going on and he knew it. Arrogance was not appealing to her, and he literally reeked of it. With all the attention he was being given from other females, Kenya couldn't understand what it was about her that he saw. She was not the one who chased behind him, nor the one that was always smiling up in his face.

If anything, she kept her distance, and didn't play into the hype. They were just friends and that's it.

When it became evident that Darius had a thing for her, girls who she once thought were her friends stopped talking to her. At one point, even Pepper was giving her shade. Every chance Pepper had, she was sure to share with Kenya some dirt she had heard about Darius and some other girl.

"Girl, don't you be letting Darius gas your head up. All he does is get into a girl's head, get the panties, and move on." Kenya never knew that side of him. She and Darius were cool, and if anything, he was the total opposite of everything she had ever heard about him. As arrogant as he was, he'd never came at her foul and had always treated her with the utmost respect. She couldn't speak on how he may have been with other girls; she only knew how he treated her.

She had been so lost in her thoughts, that she hadn't realized her phone was ringing.

"Hello."

"Do you like what you see?"

"I'm sorry," she was thrown off by the question and the sexy voice on the other end.

"It's me, Darius."

"Oh, Darius, I'm sorry, I was just looking around and got lost in my thoughts."

"So those looks weren't for me? I'm disappointed, again." He said laughing

"To be honest, I was somewhat thinking of you." She smiled.

"Really, now, we must discuss this further over dinner tonight."

"Tonight may be a stretch being that this is my first night here, but how about tomorrow night?" She asked, remembering wanting to escape the intenseness of his gaze earlier. His grayish-green eyes could make a woman melt. All he had to do is say the right thing at the wrong time, and it would be on.

"Tomorrow night, yeah, I am available." He said.

"Good, umm, call me tomorrow and let's set a time, okay? I'll leave the place up to you," She said, flustered, moving the hair out of her face.

"Cool. I heard about a new restaurant that just opened I've been wanting to try. I hope you like seafood."

"I do. I can't wait. I'll see you tomorrow."

Kenya ended their call and was preparing to make two others. She had been there for quite some time and had not called her parents, nor her best friend, letting them know she had made it there safely. Her parents didn't waste any time asking about her flight, and about her grandparents. She told them her flight was fine, and everyone was doing well. Kenya's mother was planning to visit them next month, but unfortunately, when she arrived, Kenya would be back home. She would only be there for a week or so. As a nurse, whenever she had an opportunity to get away on vacation, she did. Her goal was to go somewhere twice a year. Since she lived in D.C. and her parents lived in Sacramento, she decided to split her trips between her parents and grandparents. So far, it had worked out. This impromptu trip was the first in a while. It had been years since she had last visited Birmingham. Every time she wanted to come here, her grandparents would make their request to come there. Kenya's family was scattered all over the U.S. Her brother, Malcolm, lived in Miami, and her twin sisters, Madison and Morgan, lived in New York. Despite the distance, they always found their way to their parents' home for the holidays.

Her last phone call was going to be a good one.

"It's about darn time you called me!" Her best friend yelled in the phone.

"You know I was going to call you. How's my Pooh-bear?" Kenya asked about her Bichon Frise.

"That little yapping dog of yours is fine. Melvin and the kids are out walking him now. You know, I still believe you and my family have plotted against me with this pet business. The kids won't stop asking when they'll be getting one of their own. I so blame you for this."

"Just give in and become a fur-parent," Kenya said, laughing.

"I am a real parent. Who works constantly, plus Melvin wouldn't be any help. He's just as busy as I am. The kids don't realize how much work and dedication is required to have a pet. Our dog would call PETA on us for neglect and abandonment. Between us working and them having homework and soccer practice, I really don't see it."

"That's why they have pet daycares and walkers. My Pooh-bear is in a good one, too."

"Are you seriously on this phone talking to me about putting a dog in daycare and hiring a dog walker?"

"I was just simply pointing out how it is very doable."

"Only you would do such a thing. Will you please get married and have some children, for Christ's sake! You're that type of person to leave all your money and worldly possessions to your pet in a will, I swear, Ken." Trinity sighed. "Thousands of people could be in need, but the dog has all the money."

"Whatever! Anyway, listen, do you remember me telling you about this guy that lived across the street from my grandparents when I was growing up?"

"Talking about the one who you described, and I quote you as saying, "Panty dropper *fine* fine. Yeah, what about him?" She asked.

"What would you say if I told you he and I are planning on having dinner tomorrow night, and that time has been very, very, and I do mean very, good to him?"

"I'd say your fast tail is playing with fire, and your butt need to stay far away from him before you mess up."

They both laughed.

"Where did you run into him?'

"He's was standing across the street when I arrived, and helped Papa with my luggage."

"Details...Details?" She inquired.

"I don't have any yet, but when I do, I'll give you a call," Kenya promised.

"Now for the latest news in your love saga. Girl, Stephen has been blowing my phone up.

It's driving him crazy that he doesn't know where you are."

"Good. Stephen's the one that said maybe we should see other people."

"He only said that because of your hesitancy in accepting his marriage proposal. Girl, he is losing it. I thought he was going to punch Dr.

Colby in the face yesterday. Colby being Colby, made some sly remark about Stephen needing to have his head in surgery and not somewhere else. Thank God it was just the three of us scrubbing out. It took all I had to hold him back. He is really flipping out, Ken. I think you should call him, at least let him know you're okay."

"You're such a softy, but I'm not calling him anytime soon. I'll call him when I get back."

"Ken, that's a week from now!"

"Yeah, I know, but I need time to think about this. He proposed three weeks ago. He has yet to allow me to think about things. This is something I really need to work out." She whispered in the phone. "I've heard every message he has left. It was one desperate plea after another. My mind hasn't changed. Being away will give me a chance to really think about it."

"Do you love him, Ken?"

"I do. I really do. This has nothing to do with Stephen, but everything to do with me."

"Well, have you told him that?"

"Countless times. He is so convinced it's about him, and it isn't."

"Ken, please call him and let him know you're okay. Don't do this to him. They're back from walking the dog, so I'll talk to you later. Call him, Ken."

"I'll think about it," Kenya playfully told her.

"You better. Love you, bye."

Trinity and Kenya had become the best of friends when they were assigned to be roommates their freshmen year at Howard University. They had almost everything in common. The girls even pledged the same sorority together. Kenya was so proud of her best friend, who graduated at the top of her class, and had become a successful surgeon. It was Trinity who introduced Stephen to Kenya a year ago, and after dating for six months, they had begun to talk about marriage. Stephen was everything that Kenya had prayed and asked God about, and more. He had secretly planned to pop the question, but his five-year-old niece spoiled it. Lexa looked just like a baby doll. She had naturally loose curls that bounced below her shoulders as she played. Playfully, she came up to Kenya and asked her if she could wear her princess dress to her party. Confused, Kenya asked her, "What party, sweetheart?"

Little girl responded with a giggle and said, "You know, the one where Uncle Stephen gives you your ring."

Shocked, she didn't know what to say. Her eyes automatically connected with Stephen's. All of a sudden, she felt overwhelmed. So many thoughts were running through her mind at once. Someone else would hop at the chance to marry Stephen. This handsome Trinidadian native came from a well to do family of physicians. He moved here with his parents thirty years ago. She loved his family's dynamic. They were so loving and supportive of one another, and they welcomed her into their hearts the moment they met her. On the car ride back to her apartment, she hadn't spoken two words to Stephen. So he broke the silence between them.

"Baby, I hope that you aren't disappointed about learning of my surprise. I had so many things planned out. Ugh, that little girl!" He shouted in frustration. "But since you know of my intentions, what are your thoughts?"

"I have so many thoughts. I wouldn't know where to begin."

"I was hoping for an expression of excitement. You look worried and afraid. What's wrong?"

"It's a lot to consider. I am going to need some time before I can give-"

"Time! Kenya, I'm asking you to spend the rest of your life with me, baby, or at least this is what I'm hoping to do."

"Yes, I know. I just really want to think about some things. I am not saying no. I am only saying I need time to think."

"Think as you will woman, but know you are my rib." She heard him say in his Caribbean accent that drove her crazy.

Chapter 6

This was the main reason for coming to Birmingham. Looking at Stephen had a way of clouding Kenya's judgment. Kenya could be strong-willed at times, and he knew her weaknesses. This was a major life-altering decision. She knew compromise was something that would be required if she planned on becoming Stephen's wife. Stephen had mentioned to her his desire of wanting to move back to Trinidad if he had a chance, to open a clinic in his city, Port of Spain. He told her how it would be a great place to raise a family, and how he'd love to show her his family home there. She had only seen pictures of this beautiful estate. He spoke of his country with such love, excitement, and passion. But to leave hers behind with everything she loved, her family and friends, would be too difficult for her to do. Her family was either a flight or a train away. Not to take into account the very long hours he already spent at the hospital, what would she do in a foreign country? Had Stephen given Kenya the opportunity to properly explain why she was hesitant, he wouldn't have jumped to conclusions. To assume she would want to be with someone else was simply absurd. She just needed a chance to share her thoughts and heart with him.

Kenya, still, was nobody's fool. She knew what she had in Stephen, and she wasn't about to give him up for anything. She knew they needed to talk, and talk they would, soon.

Before she unpacked, Kenya went to check on her grandparents. She found her grandmother in the kitchen making coffee, and her grandfather in his den watching one of those cowboy shoot 'em up pictures. She went back to her room and unpacked her clothes.

The aroma of the coffee not only filled her room but nostrils too. It invited her to have a cup, and she accepted the offer. While in the kitchen, she heard the doorbell ring, and her grandmother speaking to someone. While fixing her coffee, she noticed that there were different flavors of coffee syrup on the counter. Impressed, she drizzled caramel syrup in her coffee and went to find her grandmother.

Kenya found her sitting on the front porch with Ms. Alfreda.

"Hey, Ms. Alfreda," she spoke, then giving her a welcoming hug. She then touched her grandmother's shoulder, saying, "I didn't know you were a Barista, Granny," after taking another sip of her coffee.

"Oh no child, your grandmother is a Baptist, we all are," Alfreda stated.

"Huh?" Kenya asked, confused.

"Um-hmm, we sure are. I remember when I first got baptized as a child." Birdie said.

"Yeah, we don't do those strange religions." Alfreda agreed.

"Uh uh, we sholl don't, honey." Birdie said, rocking back and forth with her arms folded.

"But...never mind." Kenya did not have enough coffee nor the energy to adequately explain to them what a Barista was.

She sat her favorite coffee cup down and asked Alfreda about her old childhood friend, Pepper.

"Oh, Pepper is doing good. She lives in Florida now. Those three boys she has keep her going. They just move so much by her husband being in the military."

"Lawd, that girl is living in Florida running behind them peanut head boys. They took those heads after their grandfather." Birdie commented.

Trying not to laugh, Kenya responded best she could. "That's great, Ms. Alfreda. The next time you talk to her, please tell her that I said hello."

"I sure will." Alfreda said, cutting her eyes at Birdie. "Well, honey, how is life treating you up there in D.C.? You're looking good. Somebody is keeping you happy, I see." She teased her.

"Thank you, Ms. Alfreda. Everything is good. I have no complaints."

"Your grandmother talks about you and your doctor beau all the time. You should've brought him with you."

Awkwardly, Kenya responded, "Maybe next time." She said, taking a sip of her coffee.

Alfreda noticed the tension in her body. "Young lady let this old woman give you some womanly advice. I know you didn't ask me, but I'm telling you anyway because I wished somebody had told this old fool. If you have a good man that loves you, I mean one that is truly concerned about your well-being, and he honors you by placing your needs before his own, this is a man worth keeping. I made the worst mistake of my life by not valuing what I had. Please, don't make that same mistake." Alfreda told her.

"Yes ma'am," Kenya replied, trying hard to force back her tears.

Walter broke the silence when he called Birdie's name. "Birdie, your pot is boiling over, and George said he was going to stop by to see Kenya," he told her.

"Oh Lawd, I forgot I had something on the stove. Well, did you at least move the pot off the eye, or turn my greens down?" She asked, jumping up.

"Abrams," Alfreda spoke.

"Alfreda." He said with a slight smile before answering his wife. "Yeah, Birdie, I did. You out here about to burn my house down being nosey as usual." He said, grumbling and returning in the house.

"Well, Sir Jesus. He hadn't cracked a smile at me in years, months of Sundays. That's it! Get your soul right, church. The world is coming to an end." Alfreda said fanning with one of those church fans that had the funeral home's advisement on it.

Birdie stepped back outside just in time to watch the local glass repairman arrive.

"It's a doggone shame that girl did that to his car," Alfreda said.

"He deserved it, and a lot more if you ask me." Birdie responded. "Bringing all that drama to his parent's house, and you know they gonna find out."

"Um-hmm, if they haven't already. You know folks say we nosey, but Maxine Mosely got us beat." Alfreda stated.

"Girl, don't she stay peeping out that window, and you better believe she don't miss a beat either, baby."

"I know that's right!" Alfreda shouted. "But Birdie, she can tell folks everything else, but how she dress up in all them funny looking wigs and sunglasses to go to the liquor store?"

Hmph, as if don't nobody know it's her. Lady, stop yo mess! Everybody knows that's you. What are you hiding for?"

"Say what, now?" Kenya asked, laughing.

"Girl, yeah! She wears all kinds of disguises. All because she's afraid of someone from the church seeing her go inside. Chile, don't nobody care about that."

"Sure, don't! Freda, you remember that day she left both her money and the liquor at the store trying to get away from us?" Birdie asked, laughing.

"Honey, yes! I'll never forget that day. See, Kenya, your grandmother and I was in there looking for some Jack Daniels to make my cold remedy medicine, and honey, here she come tipping through there in one of those tore up wigs and dark shades. She was looking around so hard, that she looked clean past us. Next thing we know, she snatched up some Wild Turkey and sashayed to the counter. We were standing in line right behind her, when you know who said hey

Maxine," she said, pointing at Birdie. "Baby, before we knew it, Maxine Mosley flew up out of there," Alfreda said, barely talking through her laughter. "Girl, that thang nearly broke her neck trying to leave so fast. But here's what makes it so funny. Your grandmother wasn't even talking to her, but the cashier on the next register. Until this very day, every time I see Maxine, I chuckle."

"And she quick to say the liquor ain't for her, but the company at her house." Birdie added, rolling her eyes.

"Well, if that's the case, why can't her company get their own alcohol?" Kenya asked.

"That's an answer we all would like to know," Alfreda said, laughing. "I'll tell you this much. You should be real in everything you do. All that fake mess is unnecessary. All those airs will get you caught up every time. I look at it like this. If you drink, you drink, and if you don't, you don't. Don't go around looking like no fool trying to dip and dodge people; be you. "

"You betta say that, Freda!" Birdie added.

"But get this, Kenya. Your messy grandmother, my dearest friend, had nothing else better to do, with her petty self, but to take that woman her change and Wild Turkey that she left behind."

"Granny, what?" Kenya asked.

"Well she said that it was for her company, why should they suffer." She said, smirking.

"Girl, that woman was too embarrassed to even open the door, and we knew she was at home because her car was in the driveway. So this fool right here writes a note on the envelope saying, "You left your money and package." She then put them both in the mailbox. It's a really good thing that the postman had already ran for that day."

"Granny, you are something else," Kenya said, laughing.

"She sure is. Ask Petty Betty why she used one of those tithe and offering envelopes from the church to do it?"

Laughing, Birdie responded, "Because that was the only envelope I could find at the time. I'm not thinking about Messy Bessie over there. I wasn't about to go rambling through no drawers looking for nothing. All I wanted was for the woman to get her money and package back, and she did."

"Yeah, right," Alfreda said side-eyeing Birdie. "Then she has the nerve, Kenya, to wonder why that woman won't halfway speak to her," Alfreda said, laughing. "She knows exactly why."

"Chile, whatever. Ain't nobody thinking about her and that foolishness," Birdie said, waving the foolishness away. "But I bet you'll never guess who I saw the other day at the grocery store?" Birdie asked Alfreda.

"Who?" Alfreda asked, all anxious.

"Your best friend, Loretta, and her oldest daughter Christina." She said, laughing knowing full well Alfreda couldn't stand that woman.

"Hmph, I thought you had seen somebody. Besides, I haven't seen that wench since the day she tried to accuse my grandbaby, Pepper, of stealing money out of her wallet."

"I remember that! It turned out, it was her very own granddaughter who done it."

"Girl yeah, talking about twenty dollars, and she only had two dollars in there to start. A

bunch of crooks if you ask me. That whole family crooked, especially the youngest boy, what's his name. That boy would steal sugar out of a pound cake."

"They say Christopher isn't like that anymore. I hadn't seen him since his dad's funeral, and it was so sad. Freda, you must admit that nothing was sadder than seeing that boy at Peter's funeral. It broke my heart to hear Christopher cry out for his dad like that."

"Yes, it was. If it weren't for me having to usher, you know I wouldn't have been there, but I was glad to see that Loretta wasn't. But then again we *are* talking about the same woman who called herself going to leave this man she was staying with, only to move back in a day later. Kenya, I kid you not, this woman had packed up a whole house. Who does that?"

"Maybe she realized she was wrong and came back," Kenya offered as an explanation. "Chile please, you mean she came back because she had nowhere else to go," Alfreda said.

"Freda, I'm telling you the truth, funerals are not my thing, but losing his father did something to him. You remember when Red died and how his kids acted a stone fool at his funeral?"

"Girl, yeah. I never seen folks cut up so bad in all my life."

"Kenya, it was a shame girl. All of Red's children got to fighting with each other, right there at the gravesite. You know it started during the funeral service when they were trying to sit up front with the other family," Birdie said.

"But why, Granny? I don't understand. If they were his children as well, why wouldn't they be allowed to sit with the rest of the family?"

"They would have had they not been thirty minutes late."

"Who does that?" Alfreda asked again. "Who would show up late to their own parent's funeral?"

"Girl, it was an absolute mess, wasn't it Freda? Pastor got them to all calm down at the church, but baaaby, when they hit that cemetery, it was on."

"It sure was. Kenya. I remember when your Granny was almost six feet deep herself fooling around with them folks herself." Alfreda said tickled.

"What?!" Kenya shouted.

"Alfreda, that mess ain't funny." Birdie told her while rolling her eyes.

"Yes, it was too. Let me tell you, Kenya. While all the commotion was going on, the First
Lady decided she would help out by pulling people apart. Honey, I don't know who it was, but they were fighting so hard, they knock her back, and she was trying to grab hold on to anyone she could to keep from falling. Guess who she tried to grab?" Freda asked, pointing her finger at Birdie. "Baby, your Granny moved clean out of the way, and down went Frazier, wig and all."

"Granny, you didn't!" Kenya asked in shock.

"Granny, nothing!" Birdie responded. "She wasn't about to knock me down. I'm too old to fall. She'd heal up quicker than I eva would. Hmph, I wasn't thinking about her. Ain't nobody told her to go over there and pull nobody apart, anyway. She should have minded her own business like I was doing."

"You could've at least helped her up, Birdie."

"Why? I didn't help her get down there. Pastor came over and helped her up, and that was good enough for me."

Kenya couldn't help but laugh while she was sat back, enjoying her coffee, and listening to more of the latest neighborhood gossip. The only other person missing out of this scenario was Pepper. They would sit on these very steps as little girls and get an ear full. It was a good place to be until Pepper would chime in on their conversation, and like always, one of them would tell her to stay out of grown folks business, but that didn't stop her from spreading the little tidbits she had heard with the others.

Pepper was careful not to repeat the stories of the parents of the kids present. She would wait until they were all gathered together on Sundays to hold her special gossip session. On the back pew of Mt. Zion Baptist Church, she recalled some of the wildest stories she'd ever heard.

She remembered hearing about the time Alecia's mother, Ms. Mary, snatched a wig off some woman's head for cheating with her husband. How Pepper told the story, the lady's hair wasn't longer than a second. She also told them about Edgar's dad, who claimed to have hurt his back at work and was photographed by the insurance company when he was caught up on the ladder cleaning out the gutters. Then to make matters worse, when Mr. King realized he had been photographed, he fell off the ladder hurting his back for real. He tried to sue the company for invasion of privacy, but didn't win. Then she told them about the time Tyler Griggs's brother Sam got caught selling hot meat to people out of the trunk of his car. When the police questioned him about where he had gotten the meat from, he told them out of the dumpster. Which at the

time was not a lie, because Marcus's sister Ebony had been the one putting it out there. They were robbing Shop and Go Grocery blind. Needless to say, when they found out, they redirected Ebony's career path.

As the ladies sat there laughing and talking, a black Harley - Davidson cruiser pulled into the driveway, capturing their attention.

"Looks like you have more company visiting, Granny."

"You sure do Birdie," Alfreda said, smiling because she knew who it was.

"Oh, that's your Uncle George. He knows he's too old to be still riding that thang, making all that noise in the neighborhood. Let me get up and let Walter know he's out here. As if he hadn't heard him coming a mile away." Birdie said, walking to the door. "Walt, George is out here!" she yelled.

Finally, making it to the steps of the front porch in all black, boots, Levi's, t-shirt, and his motorcycle club vest, he greeted them with the warmest smile. Birdie's youngest brother, Deacon George Watson, had the women of the church swooning. He was one of the good ones, and she couldn't be more proud of him. You never heard a single bad thing about him or his family. Even after his wife passed, women were throwing themselves at him left and right, but he paid them no attention. A good looking, charming man like himself could have anyone, but he spent the majority of his time either with his family, riding his bike, or fishing. At first, Birdie

was worried about him and didn't know how he would get along with Rose being gone, but as it turns out, he was doing well. She often wondered if he would marry again, but never pushed the subject like their other sister did. Birdie felt that George would make that step in due time, and if he didn't, that was okay too. All she wanted was for him to be happy and safe, but that motorcycle had to go. Now that was her issue to push, and it wasn't safe at his age, she thought.

"I see you riding on that death trap today."

"Well, hello to you too, sister," he said, ignoring her. "Is that my favorite great-niece sitting over there?" He asked, smiling at Kenya.

"Yeah, that's our baby." Birdie proudly answered.

"Little Kenya! Oh, my goodness. Girl, give your old uncle a hug. Lawd have mercy. I haven't seen this child in years." He said, hugging her lovingly. "I hear so many great things about you and your siblings from Maw and Paw over there. They are so proud of you all, and so am I," he told her. "My favorite sister, I need a favor. Will you please make us one of your delicious peach cobblers for next week's meeting? You know nobody makes them like you and mama," he complimented her.

Flattered, "Whenever y'all want one, George, just call me, and I'll make it for you." Birdie told him. "But does our other sister know that I'm your favorite today?" She asked him, being messy. George always had a favorite this or that. To be honest, everything and everyone was his favorite.

"Nope, not today. She has been running me like crazy for the past couple of days. She's getting her kitchen remodeled, and every day, we're looking at something new. Shoot, I'm tired."

"Well, you know our sister," is all Birdie had to offer because she was glad that Annette hadn't called her to go. That woman could shop 'til she dropped, literally.

Yes, I do, but hopefully, she's done. Bird, if you really love now, and care about your favorite brother, please don't forget about us next week. No offense to anyone," he said, "But if I have to eat one more piece of that dry pound cake Sister Patterson sends us, I don't know what I'll do." He told them.

The porch erupted in laughter. The look of disgust and disappointment on his face made them laugh even harder. Birdie and Alfreda knew all too well about Barbara Patterson's pound cake. They won't forget how much she brags about her famous pound cake that everyone is so crazy about.

"We understand, George. Her pound cake should come with a warning label that says will choke if swallowed," Birdie said.

"I know that's right. I have never had a piece of cake that scraped my throat going down," Alfreda said, clearing and rubbing her throat from the horrible memory.

"That's why Brother Patterson brings all that water with him to the Deacon's meetings. It finally makes sense. Umph umph umph," he said, shaking his head. "Well, anything you can do, Sis, I appreciate it. I'm getting ready to roll out. Ms. Alfreda, it's always good seeing you."

"I see somebody forgot to wear their eyeglasses today," Walter commented.

"Walter!" Birdie shouted.

"Oh, pay him no attention, darling. Grandpa Grumpy over there just mad because he's not as sweet as me. Don't worry, Grumpy; I'll be leaving soon enough."

Before Walter could make another smart remark, the glass falling from the windshield captured all of their attention.

"Looks like a rock got him," George said.

"More like a girl throwing a brick got him," Alfreda told him.

"What...Umph, umph, umph." He said, shaking his head. "Well, let me roll on that note. I was just stopping by on my way to club meeting to see my favorite girl. I'll see y'all tomorrow at church. Baby girl, it was so good seeing you." He said, taking her hands and giving them a gentle squeeze.

"I'll see you later, George," Walter said before returning inside.

Before cranking up his motorcycle, George wanted to tell Darius this one thing. "Don't sweat it, Youngblood. I've had a brick or two thrown in my day, too."

Although Darius was annoyed as hell that this man knew his business, he couldn't help but to give the guy respect with a grin and a head nod. He looked like he had it going on back in the day, and could still get into some trouble today.

"Man, that brother's bike is cold," Jay said.

"As ice. Did you check out those pipes? He makes me want to pull mine out." "You know I did. I've always wanted one, but you know who had a problem with it." "Oh, let me guess. Carmen," Darius replied, rolling his eyes.

"No, man! Anyway. It was my mama. You act like I don't have a mind of my own when it comes to Carmen. I do what I want to do."

"Is that right? So you are coming to RJ's bachelor's party in Atlanta next weekend, then?" Darius asked him.

"Ah, ah, you know. Um, if everything's straight here, then yeah, but ah, you know how things come up. So yeah, we'll see."

"Just like I thought. You're not coming," Darius told him, laughing and taking another sip.

"Man, whatever. It's not what you think," Jay said, trying to defend himself. "You just don't understand, man."

"You right, I don't, and at the moment, I don't care. As far as I'm concerned, all of this right here," he said, waving his hands, "is Carmen's fault."

"Dee, I *know* we not about to get into this all over again, man?"

"Go ahead and take up for her like you always do, but we both know the truth, no matter what you say."

Chapter 7

It was never a dull moment in their neighborhood, and when Kenya looked across the street at Darius's car, the drama continued. She couldn't relate to his drama, but she had some of her own to hammer out. Kenya was thankful for the advice Ms. Alfreda had given her. It was exactly what she needed to hear. She thought back to her family and how everyone loved Stephen, especially her grandmother. Their meeting would be one she would never forget.

Kenya's grandparents had come to visit her in D.C. It wasn't hard to do since, at that time,

President Obama was in office. She didn't know if they were more excited to see her or to tour the White House. If her grandmother thought they'd allow her to walk right up to the front door without being shot down, she would have. Her grandparents were so proud of him, and in their eyes, he could do no wrong.

Their visit was so special that Stephen had taken off from work just to meet and spend time with them. In all of her 28 years of life, Kenya had never seen her grandfather jealous of another man, but on this day, she had. Kenya made the usual introductions, and when Stephen said hello beautiful to her grandmother, it had gone downhill from there. Her grandmother stood in the middle of Ronald Reagan Washington National Airport with the biggest Colgate smile she'd ever seen in her life. She overheard her grandfather ask, "Birdie, do you think you can smile any harder and walk at the same time? I'm ready to go," he asked, rolling his eyes. She was not phased one bit. Later that day, Kenya teased Stephen about putting the moves on her grandmother.

Since that time, they had all become very close. It was nothing for Stephen to call and talk to her grandparents. That's why if her grandmother had an inkling she had been sitting there thinking about not marrying Stephen, she would slap her natural curls straight. Kenya could hear

her saying, "Girl, I know you have lost your mind now. Are you crazy?" The good news was only she and Trinity knew what was going on.

It was time that she faced the music. She excused herself and went back into the house to go to her room. She picked her phone up and saw that she had yet another missed call from Stephen. Kenya took a deep breath and called him back.

Without saying hello, Stephen immediately apologized. "Kenya, I am so sorry. I didn't mean to assume-"

"No, honey, it was me," Kenya said, speaking low as she closed her bedroom door.

"Where are you? I came by. Your next-door neighbors said they saw you leave this morning."

"Yeah, I am visiting my grandparents."

"Grandparents! Kenya, you-" Stephen semi-speechless, couldn't quite get his words out.

"You mean to tell me that you left the city because of our disagreement?" He asked.

"I left because I needed to think, and I couldn't do that as long as you were around."

"Kenya, what are you saying? Do you not want us to be together?"

"Stephen, of course, I want to be with you! I love you! I just needed time to think about some things."

"What is there to think about, baby? You love me, and I love you. Is that not enough?"

"It is more than enough. The problem is..." Kenya tried to explain while fighting back the tears and a lump in her throat.

"Kenya?"

Sniffling, she continued, "To marry you would mean to leave my family behind."

"What do you mean, why would you think that?"

"You said it has always been your dream to move back to your country to raise a family and open a clinic. To do that would mean to leave everyone behind. It's selfish of me, I know but-."

"Kenya, if you ever heard me say that, then how did you miss the part of me also saying this was once a dream of mine as a child. Besides, I would never place you in a position to ever have to choose. Even if this was my dream, I would discuss it with you first. If it were the other way around baby, and you wanted to move to the west coast, I'd make it happen. Why? Because

I love you that much, and if you loved me that much, it wouldn't matter just as long as we were together; Saturn couldn't be far enough. I understand your closeness with your family. I am close to mine as well. But for you, I'd make that sacrifice," He said, sighing. "It has to be more to it because your family lives all over the country, so baby talk to me, what is your hesitation?"

"To be honest, I really don't know, but I do regret ever hurting you. I didn't mean to. I just wanted enough time to get my thoughts together."

"When are you coming home?" He asked, sternly.

Hearing the aggravation in his tone, she replied, "I'm scheduled to leave next Saturday."

"Ok, so I'll see you next week then? I'll talk to you later."

"Wait...don't end our call like this."

"You left me to think, right? So I don't want to waste any more of your time."

"I don't want us to say good-bye this way. You're angry and-"

"Anger does not describe how I feel right now. I would love to be angry. Try disappointed, and hurt," he said, then ending their call.

Devastated, Kenya laid across her bed and sobbed silently until she fell asleep.

Chapter 8

Kenya woke up to the fragrance of bacon and fresh coffee. It smelled heavenly to her, as she realized she had not eaten yesterday. She fell asleep in all her clothes last night, and before she could remove them to take a shower, her grandmother was knocking at her bedroom door.

"Come in."

"Good morning, baby. Grandma made you a big breakfast of all your favorites. You fell asleep while I was cooking dinner. You must've been tired to fall asleep in your clothes like that. I wanted to wake you up so you could at least change, but your Papa thought you needed the rest."

"Thank you, Granny, I did. Do you think you could keep everything warm while I take a quick shower?"

"Sure, baby. Go right ahead. I have to go downstairs and monitor the bacon, or else we won't have any."

"Yes, ma'am. Thank you, Granny, I appreciate you."

When she was alone, she looked at her phone for any missed messages sent by Stephen.

Her heart leaped when she saw that there was. The message sent well after midnight simply said,

"I love you more than life itself. Forgive me for my behavior." A sigh of relief had escaped her lips. She had gone to bed, knowing that she had lost him forever. They had never had a disagreement of this magnitude before, and she prayed that it would never happen again. She wanted to call him, but it was after ten there, and he'd be in church. She made plans to call him later as her stomach growled, reminding her of the need for food. She sent him a quick I love you so much text and hopped in the shower.

"Good morning, everyone!" Kenya spoke all bright-eyed and bushy-tailed.

"Hey, Baby girl! How did you sleep last night?" Her grandfather asked.

"Good, Papa."

"You know your grandma was going to wake you up, but I made her leave you alone. I told her when you've been traveling like that, going to bed dirty is the best night's rest anyone can get."

"You know you need to stop with that old wise tale. You tried to pull that mess on me back in fifty-six, but I said not in my bed you won't." Birdie said.

"Woman, what you talking bout? That's what my daddy told us coming up, and it's true."

"If it's so true, how come your mama didn't allow him to do it when he was working at the Paper Mill?"

"That's not true, Birdie. My mama said it didn't make her a bit of difference, because they had their own beds. He could go to bed how he wanted in his."

"Um-hmm, somebody got cleaned somewhere because the youngest child was born nine months later." Birdie said, making her point.

Kenya continued to laugh at her grandparents' antics. Sitting before her was fifty plus years of unconditional love. The kind of love that had been modeled throughout her life. It influenced their children and now their grandchildren. It was the same love that she believed she had found in Stephen.

Rushing to finish eating so they wouldn't be late for church, Kenya almost missed the beautiful floral bouquet sitting in the middle of the table.

"Granny, this is a beautiful floral arrangement. Was this here yesterday?"

"No, they came this morning." She said, smiling.

"Aww, look at my Papa being all romantic. You go, boy." Kenya said, teasing him.

Before Walter could say anything, Birdie chimed in, "Chile, please, Walter hadn't done anything of the sort. These came from my future grandson. Um-hmm, he loves himself some Granny baby. You have a delivery too, but yours isn't as pretty as mine." She told her, waving her fork towards the living room.

Walter was rolling his eyes at Birdie, "Anyway, Baby girl, your Granny is in here tripping as usual, like I can't send a floral arrangement, big whoop. But yours is sitting on the table waiting for you. Ms. Nosey Rosey couldn't wait for you to open your box."

Kenya excused herself from the table. She opened her box and saw the prettiest long stem red roses, but it was the card that brought tears to her eyes.

Dear Beautiful,

May we never repeat a day like yesterday.

You are my today, tomorrow, and future.

Bring my heart back to me, come home.

Love you forever,

-Stephen

Come home was exactly what she was going to do. She checked the next outgoing flights to D.C. The earliest flight was a couple hours away, and she had just enough time to change her booking for that flight, and attend Sunday service with her grandparents.

Chapter 9

Kenya had to explain to them that there was a change of plans, and then she needed to get back home quickly. After church service, while sitting in an Italian Bistro, she told her grandparents that Stephen had proposed. Elated, her grandmother couldn't have been happier.

Her grandfather, on the other hand, not so much.

"Are you sure about this, Baby girl?" He asked her.

"**Walter!**" Birdie yelled.

"More than anything, Papa," Kenya answered.

"I don't know. Back in my day, the fella proposed in person on bended knee, not by a note on some flowers." He said, feeling some kind of way.

"I don't care how she got it, as long as she got it! Lawd, my baby bout to get married.

Have you told your parents yet?" Birdie asked, beaming.

"No, ma'am. No one knows besides you all and Trinity."

"Trinity?"

"Yes, Granny, Trinity."

"Well, how could she know? You just got the proposal this morning. Y'all young folks know how to send them type messages on that phone, I tell ya."

"Text messages and no ma'am." Kenya took a deep breath before proceeding, "He proposed weeks ago."

"**Weeks ago!**" Birdie shouted. People were starting to stare.

"Yes, ma'am. Because I was so hesitant, he thought I wanted to see other people, but it was all a big misunderstanding. I thought he wanted to move us to Trinidad and raise a family. Something so silly caused three weeks of confusion. We had a chance to talk things out last night, and I have decided to say yes."

"Heffa, are you crazy!?" Birdie shouted. Shocked, Kenya's eyes were as big as the saucers sitting on the table, and her chin was just about on the floor.

"Birdie!" Walter shouted back.

"I wouldn't have cared if he had said y'all were moving to Timbuktu, by way of Mars and the moon, I *knew* this man loved me." Birdie said, pointing to her husband. "When you know what you have, it does not matter where you live, just as long as the two of you are together, and above anything else, it is in God's will for your life," she told her.

"The best advice I could ever give you as your grandpa is this. Whenever you are faced with a challenge in life, never run. No matter what, you must face it head-on, and together. When the two shall become one, there is no I or me. It's all about us. I could have never survived fifty years with this crazy woman sitting next to me, if all I thought about was me, and what I wanted. In all that you do, you must continue to put God first, and he will direct your path to the right decision every time." Her grandfather told her.

"I'm so glad that you finally came to your senses. I would have hated to disown you." Birdie said, teasing her, but not really.

Chapter 10

While at the restaurant, Kenya received a text message from Darius asking her about their pending dinner plans. She had forgotten about him and had to tell him about her plans to leave shortly to return home. She didn't have much to do in terms of packing. Her clothes from yesterday were just coming out of the dryer, thanks to her grandmother. Once those were folded and placed in her luggage, she was ready. She sent Stephen her flight itinerary and responded to

Darius's text, asking him to call her.

"Hey, Gorgeous, how are you?" Darius called her.

A newly engaged woman shouldn't be smiling this hard, she thought.

"I'm good Darius, how are you?"

"Better now that I get a chance to talk to you. What's up with dinner?"

"We won't be able
to go. I'm sorry."
"What! Why?" He
asked.

"I'm returning home today."

"Girl, I know dog gon' well you didn't have all that luggage for a day?"

Laughing, she said, "No, I intended to stay longer, but an issue I had was resolved, and

I'm headed back home."

"Um-hmm, let me guess you and your man had some type of falling out, he said sorry, and you forgave him. Am I right?"

"Not quite, but close. I'll give you that much."

"I hate that we didn't get a chance to catch up, though. I need to hear all about this man that stole you away from me."

"Really. From what I hear, your hands are all kinds of full."

"Let me guess. The street committee informed you on the latest gossip, huh? Don't believe everything you hear. Hey, I have a wonderful idea. Let me take you to the airport, and we'll catch up. I'll tell you all about my drama on the way."

"I don't know if Birdie and Walter will go for that. They have always seen me off." "Mr. Abrams is cooler than a fan, but that grandmother of yours, as beautiful as she is, can be a piece of work," he said, laughing. "She always gives me the blues."

"Let me discuss it with them, and I'll hit you up. Besides, I'll have to be heading out shortly anyway."

"Cool, just let me know."

It wasn't hard to convince her grandfather to let someone else drive her to the airport, but her grandmother wasn't having it, especially when she heard who was going to take her.

"But Granny, why are you acting like that?"

"Un-uh, nope. No newly engaged woman need to be riding in that pimpmobile he has."

"Granny, nothing is going to change my mind about marrying Stephen."

"Un-huh, and I'm going to make sure that it doesn't either. That boy over there is the sly, the slick, and the wicked. No Lawd, I don't know what he does to these women, but whatever it is, it ain't right. Come on, Walt, get up so we can take our baby to the airport."

"Birdie, I ain't moving from this chair. She has my blessing to go. Baby girl, please tell Darius that I said thank you for doing an old man a favor. Tell him it's ok that sly and slick ride with y'all, but leave wicked at home. Birdie has lost her mind. A pimp car, who even knows what that is, or what she is talking about." He said, shaking his head.

Her grandmother was good and mad and regretted the day she decided not to learn how to drive, then her husband had the nerve to quote that Lost Generation song trying to be funny.

"Baby, you know you can take a cab, or maybe Alfreda can take you? Oh shoot, I just remembered Alfreda went to eat dinner at her son's house. Cab it is, then."

"Birdie, that girl is not taking a cab anywhere. She has a ride right there. She'll be fine, and you will have to get over it. She is an adult, and she knows what she's doing."

"Walter Abrams, you need to stay out of other folks business." "Birdie Abrams, I've been telling you that for years."

Kenya said her good-byes to her grandparents and promised to come back with Stephen on her next visit while Darius loaded up his car with her luggage.

"Okay, Birdie, let her go, she's going to be late," Walter told her.

"Ok, ok, ok, I just got one more thang to say. Darius, make sure you take my grandbaby directly to the airport, cause if you don't and something--" was all she was able to say before being pulled in the house by her husband.

"See what I mean?" Darius said, pulling out of the driveway.

"I see. What I don't understand is why?"

"I'm not sure. I think it all started in my teenage years."

"Oh, I get it now. That's the time you called yourself crushing on me and others too."

"Nah, see, you got it all wrong, girl. I really liked you, but they really liked me." "If you say so," Kenya said through her laughter.

"I'm so serious," he said convincingly.

"Alright, then tell me this; what happened the other day?" She asked him as he emerged on I-20 E headed toward the airport with ease in his BMW X5.

"Drama, drama, drama. I called myself looking out for one of my homegirls who had too much to drink at a party by driving her car to my parents. Long story short, another girl who I was friends with dropped by exactly when my homegirl came by to pick her car up. With their bad blood, things could've popped off anywhere, Shell gas station, McDonald's, church, the hospital, you name it."

"So, were you seeing both of these women?"

Darius paused before answering her question because he didn't want to make it seem like he was misleading these women. "I was not seeing either one of them. We were all friends from high school, that's it."

"And you are friends with both women in the same way?"

"Not really. I mean, I'm a single, good looking guy, no children, with a great career. Not that I'm boasting, but the one that I was friends with, I knew she was feeling me, but I wasn't into her like that. She's just good people, but that's about it."

"Good people? Just because you're single with no children, and employed does not give you the right to mess over women like that, Darius."

"True, but I deal with all types of women. Lately, those that approach me are very shallow. Those are the type of women that you don't date seriously, nor marry. A woman of your caliber though, is different. You are a woman of substance and standard. You marry substance, not the shallow."

"If you know this, why do you keep settling for all the wrong type of women?"

"Who says that I have? But at the same time, if there's a need, and it's being met, why push it?"

"Because it's not being handled correctly. Confusion, havoc, and chaos showed up at your parent's home, remember? Your parents' home of all places!"

"That was an unfortunate incident, but if people could mind their own business, it wouldn't have occurred," he said, exiting 129 toward Airport Boulevard. "Nothing was going on."

"I know that you are being fulfilled, but you don't have to be a dog about it. Don't you want something more, Darius?"

"To be honest with you, I hadn't given it much thought. If I should come across that kind of woman, I would, and since I'm taking you to the airport to be with your man, there goes all my hope. Once again, you've got away."

"You know what, you are full of it. Boy, if I was all that to you, you'd of came to DC to find me back then. And by the way, a real woman with standards is not interested in just being in your bed. She desires a man with a purpose, a man with a plan. Listen to me well. Your handsome face will get older, and you may not always be able to please her physically, so what you better be able to do is pray, provide, and protect her. You'd have to be a man of principle first, long before you try to step to this caliber of woman."

"Like I said, I hadn't met that type of lady yet, and it looks like I have some growing up to do," he said, parking the car.

While Kenya checked in, Darius went to take a seat near her terminal. As he waited, he replayed what Kenya had said to him. He had never taken into consideration the needs of any woman. He started to imagine how different life could really be if he had settled down. The thought of no more running games, just a straight-up monogamous relationship weighed so heavy on his mind, that he hadn't realized that Kenya had returned, and was sitting next to him.

"Darius?" Kenya called his name and bumped his arm to get his attention.

"Hey, what's up?"

"I asked you if you wanted to get some coffee since it would be a while."

"Sure, that's fine."

While they were walking, Kenya noticed how quiet Darius was and wondered why. So she asked, "Are you okay?"

"Yeah, why do you ask?"

"Because you are very quiet, and that's quite unusual for you," she said, laughing.

"What, girl whatever. I know how to be quiet sometime, but for real I was thinking about something you had said earlier, that's all."

"I hope I didn't come off too harsh."

"Nah, it's not like I hadn't heard it all before. My folks have been saying the same things for years. When are you going to settle down, is all they ever ask."

"Well?"

"Well, what? I told you, I had never thought about it like that. While you are all up in my business, have you decided on what kind of coffee you are going to order?"

"Yes, and don't change the subject, either."

Placing their orders, and sitting at a quaint table in a corner, Darius decides to turn the tables on her. "Let me ask you something. What happened with you and your man?"

"What do you mean?"

"I mean, what happened in your relationship that caused you to board a plane?"

"Well, for starters, he proposed, and there was a misunderstanding."

"I'm assuming congratulations are in order, but a misunderstanding?"

"Thank you! Well, since you are in my business now, Stephen is a great guy. He is a Trinidad native who I met through my best friend, Trinity. They are both trauma surgeons at a local hospital in D.C., so when he would talk about his country, he would make references about being a kid wanting to open up his own practice there. So rather than accept his proposal and ask him questions for clarity, I became afraid and made a horrible assumption; then told him I needed some time to think about it."

"And y'all talk about us! There are women around here that would jump at the chance. I can't ask anything with the words **will you** in the beginning. Before you can get your next word out good, they are already jumping up and down, and screaming yes."

"Well, like I said, it was a misunderstanding on my part, so that's why I'm flying back home to tell my good thing, yes."

"I am happy for you, Kenya. You must invite me to your wedding, so that I may throw some rocks... I mean rice at you all." He said, laughing.

"Whatever," she said, laughing. "I'll have to think about it. For all I know you're only coming to push up on my bridesmaids. I don't think so, buddy. Just mail me our gifts."

"I promise to be on my best behavior." Was all Darius could say before they announced her flight.

Kenya and Darius said their goodbyes. He had placed the gentlest kiss upon her forehead and watched her until she was no longer in his sight. There goes one of the good ones, he

thought. Darius turned around to leave and bumped into a young lady that he hadn't seen standing behind him. She was so beautiful, he thought.

"I'm sorry that I bumped into you."

"Oh, it's okay, I should have been watching where I was going." She confessed.

"Leaving or returning?" He asked this beautiful angel before him.

"I'm returning." She said, smiling at him.

"My bad, my name is Darius." He said, snapping out of his stare.

Giggling, she replied, "Hi, I'm Erica McQueen."

"And a queen you are." Her smile was electrifying. "I know that you just met me, and I don't want to be presumptuous, but can we exchange numbers, and possibly catch lunch or dinner sometime if you're not seeing anyone?" He had already peeped her ring finger out.

"Sure, I don't mind."

"Would tonight be too soon?" He asked in hopes of not being shot down.

"Really? Tonight?"

"Yeah, that's if you don't already have plans. Wait, I apologize. What was I thinking? You probably have plans, and then you're just flying in. I'm so sorry," he said, feeling slightly embarrassed.

"No, it's okay, really. It just caught me off guard, that's all. Normally this doesn't happen to me."

"I understand. Normally, I'm not this pressing either, but I'd love the opportunity to get to know you better. So was that a yes about tonight then?"

"Yes!"

"Great!" He replied.

Darius and Erica had been standing there laughing and talking like old friends for an hour before they finally exchanged numbers and decided on where and what time to meet. He walked her to her car that was in long-term parking and placed her luggage in the trunk of her Mercedes SLC Roadster.

"Look at you. I see you, girl, with your two-seater." He teased her.

"It's a little something-something," she said, laughing.

"Yeah, yeah, that's what they all say." He said teasingly, then giving her a big hug.

Opening her car door, he said, "I'll see you at seven. I'm heading to the store to replace a TV." "Oh, wow, what happened?" Erica asked.

"It's a long story that you wouldn't believe. Besides, I wouldn't want to run you off, not now, not ever. I'll see you soon. Drive safely." He told her as he closed the car door."

Chapter 11

After departing from the airport, Darius made a stop by the local electronic store before landing back at his parents. He had to replace his dad's television before they returned home. He still couldn't believe all that had taken place, and then these chicks still had the nerve to hit him up, but the icing on his cake was meeting Erica. She was exactly what Kenya had been talking to him about. He was thrilled when she accepted his offer to join him for dinner. There was so much he wanted to know about her. He hurried to wrap things up in the store, placed the TV on the bed of his truck, and rush backed to the west side. In his mind, he had a date with destiny and was excited about the possibilities. He couldn't recall the last time he'd ever been this excited about a woman. She could be the one, he thought.

Spending that short a period of time with Erica, he knew this woman was worth every bit of effort to get things right. They had agreed to meet at FIVE, a restaurant in Lakeview, which was perfect for him. He had just enough time to drop the television off at his parents, rush home, shower, dress, and be at the restaurant by seven. He arrived at the restaurant early enough to secure them a table.

Darius was already attracted to her, but when she walked through the doors of FIVE wearing a long off the shoulder cream-colored sundress that popped off of her glowing cocoa brown skin, it literally took his breath away. Her dreadlocks no longer were pulled up in a bun, but now hung long cascading her beautiful heart-shaped face, with the prettiest almond-shaped brown eyes he'd ever seen. Could this woman be any more beautiful than what she already was, he thought to himself. Her fragrance engulfed his nose and took away all his senses as he stood up to greet her. It was a fragrance he was unfamiliar with, but he wouldn't be surprised if she was wearing an essential oil because it suits her. She was so soulful in how she spoke and the way she moved.

"You look amazing." He complimented and embraced her with a hug.

"Thank you. You look great too!" She said, smiling at him.

During their date, they talked about their last relationships, upbringing, and where they were on their career paths. In his mind, she was amazing. The things Kenya had said were starting to sink in. The woman that sat before him was not only beautiful but intelligent as well. She was witty and sexy. She knew what she wanted out of life, and was well on her way to accomplishing it. Darius found himself thinking about what he could do to add value to her life.

Clearly, she didn't need him, but he couldn't see himself without her.

Darius walked Erica to her car and made her promise to call him when she made it home.

On the short ride back to his house to change clothes, he was rehashing their conversation. It was so hard for him to believe a woman like her could be single, but he was thankful that she was. He told her that he was single as well, and had never been in a serious relationship. He had not met anyone who inspired him to settle down until he had met her. Just meeting Erica made Darius want to see what the future held for both of them. He spared her the latest debacle that occurred a few days ago, nor did he have plans to ever go into details about it.

He wanted to showcase his best for her, not the drama that visited him.

Chapter 12

Darius called Jay to see if he would come over to help him take down the old TV and hang the new one.

"Yo, what's going on, playboy?" Jay asked as he answered the phone.

Nothing dawg, just left a date with a woman that could be the one. What do you have going on tonight? I need help with rehanging the TV, man."

"Say what!? I'm sorry, I must be hearing things. Could you repeat that, please?"

"You heard me the first time, man. I need help with hanging the TV. You know that's a two-person job."

"Nah, not that part, the first part, because if I believed with what I thought I heard you say, I must be tripping. 'Cause it sounded like you said you found the one."

"Like I said, you heard me right, but uh, what about hanging that TV, though?"

"Dawg, you're not going to skate pass what I heard you say. I got you on the TV, but first things first. Not you, Mr. love 'em and leave 'em."

"Cool, but dude, real talk. I'm so serious. This woman is everything to me, or as much as I know about her, she is." Darius said, laughing.

"As long as we've been best friends, I've never heard you describe a woman in such a way."

"Yeah, man, I know. She just does something for me. I can see forever with this woman."

"Man, I don't know what to say. I mean, I'm at a real loss for words," Jay said, suppressing his own laughter.

"Now that's what I call a first. You're never at a loss for words," Darius said, laughing.

Jay told Darius that it would be tomorrow evening when he would be able to help with the TV. Darius figured that would be cool since his parents weren't due to come back until Wednesday; that meant they had two days to get it done.

Chapter 13

His Monday was long, but thoughts of Erica helped him to make it. He had enjoyed their long conversation the night before, talking about how they both enjoyed each other's company, and made plans to do lunch tomorrow.

Darius had just pulled into his parent's driveway when his phone rung from an unknown number.

"Hello."

"Hello."

"Hello. Who is this?"

"As if you don't know," she said.

"Moet?" He asked, frustrated.

"The one and only."

"Girl, bye. Unless you are calling me about when I can pick up my money for my window being broken, we have nothing else to discuss."

"I'm not about to give you a dime. You brought all this on yourself."

"How? I was minding my own business. Anyway, I was busy before you called me, so like I said, if this isn't about my money, I'm out."

"Whatever! See, that's your problem. You think people are supposed to cater to you." "I don't think anything. You were the one who was in the wrong and got all into your feelings, not me. We were friends, nothing more." As he was talking, he noticed that someone had just pulled up in front his parents' house, and had just cut their lights off. "Moet, did you just pull-up uninvited yet again?"

"You're about to see now, won't you." She said, hanging the phone up.

Angry, he shouted, **"What are you doing here!?"** as she exited her car.

"Oooh, Walt! Alfreda is gonna hate she missed this! That Moet girl from up the street is back!" Birdie said, peeping out of the window. Hearing yelling caused her to look out the window. That's when she noticed Darius and Moet outside in a heated argument.

"Birdie come out of that window, and mind your own business for once."

"I am minding my own business, Walt. How about you change that light bulb in the hall,

I've only been asking you to change it now for the past couple of days."

"I told you I was going to change that light bulb. You don't have to keep harping on it." "Un-huh, if I didn't, you'd never do anything. Woo, get him, girl! Yeah, Walt, she's giving him a piece of her mind." Birdie told him.

"I wished you would have a piece of mind to come out of the window," he mumbled. "What was that you said, Walt?" She turned to ask, but he had already left the room. "Walt, you had better come and see this. She's all in his face and everything. Walt! I think your buddy over there is about to get his butt whooped. That'll teach him about cheating on people. Uh-oh, Walt! She went back to her car. Wait, is she leaving? Alfreda is going to hate she missed this." She told her husband, giving him a play by play. "I wonder what that was she just took out of her car. **Is that a gun!?**" She shouted.

POP! POP! POP!

"**Walt! I've been shot! Call 911!**" Walter rushed into the living room to find his wife lying on the floor. "Walter, they done shot an innocent old woman. I hadn't harmed a soul, and yet I was the one that got the stray bullet. Lawd, Walt must be in shock, he's just standing there frozen, watching me die. **Help me! Somebody help me I've been shot!** She screamed at the top of her lungs.

Seconds later, she heard banging on the door. "Hurry, go to the door, it's the police." Walter opened the door to have Darius rush right past him.

"Oh, my God! Ms. Birdie, we heard you screaming that you had been shot." Darius said, kneeling over her.

"You ought to know! Y'all were the ones that did it!" "**What?!** We hadn't shot anybody." Moet said.

"Yes you did too, I'm laying here bleeding out, about to hold hands with Jesus because one of y'all shot me, and I am going to tell the police everything!" She said, holding her chest. "Huh?" Darius asked, confused.

"The police! Lady, you must be outta yo raggedy mind. We haven't shot anybody, and with what gun?" Moet argued.

"**Yes, you did! Walt! Tell 'em they shot me!**"

"Un-uh Darius. See what she ain't gonna do is say we shot nobody", Moet said as she whipped out her phone. "No way are you about to sit here and blame me."

Darius turned to her and asked, "Moet, what are you doing?" This is not the time to be texting anybody, he thought.

"Nawl, see, you can stand around here looking crazy if you want to. I'm about to clear my name. Hmph, think it's a game if you want to partna."

"Clear your name? What!? Moet, we haven't done anything."

"I know we haven't, and now everyone else does too."

"**Birdie, get up off the floor, fool! I dropped three damn lightbulbs in the hall!**"

"**What!**" She said, patting down her body to see if it was true. "Little girl, what are you talking about? What do you mean everyone else knows? Knows what!?" Birdie yelled quickly, getting up off of the floor.

Before Birdie could continue her interrogation, Walter had brought her a bath robe and was trying to hand her his phone at the same time. "I told you to stay out of that window, and mind your own business anyway, but noooo," he said.

"She did have a gun I saw her. She went to her car and got it."

"No, ma'am. I went to my car to give this bastard- I mean this man his money for breaking his window." Moet told her.

"Walter, now, I don't have time to be talking on that phone just yet," She said, trying to refuse the phone. "My nerves are bad and everything, but if this heffa done told my business to somebody, she's gonna be the one who needs to call somebody for help."

"Birdie, take the phone because they aren't gonna stop calling."

She sighs and takes the phone, "Hello, hello, who is this?!" She yells in the phone. "Kenya? Baby, Granny is gonna have to call-" she said before being cut off. "I'm not doing anything." She tells her. "Well, I thought they had-. Wait a minute! Did your grandfather call you and tell you this? Facebook!" She yelled. "Heffa, I'm about to kill you!" She said, leaping at Moet.

Thank God for Darius. He caught Birdie mid-air and was completely shocked by her strength. This little old woman was about to tear Moet a new one. "**Moet, why did you do that?!**" Darius yelled at her.

"Because she said we shot her, and I'm not about to be blamed for nothing."

"You can clearly see she's not shot, and you know we hadn't done anything?" He said, still wrestling to hold Birdie. "Ms. Birdie, can you please calm down?"

"I ain't got to do nothing, but whoop her butt. **Turn me a loose, boy!**" She yelled, trying to get out of his grip. "What you don't do little girl is talk out of my house. Turn me loose, Darius. I ain't playing with you, or her. This gone be my last time telling you, too."

Walter, fully annoyed, picked his phone up, and told his granddaughter he'd call her back once everything had settled down. Then he walked over to Darius and told him to release Birdie, and to take Moet home.

Darius did as he was told, praying Walter was just as strong as he was.

"Come on, Moet, let's go." He told her while standing between her and Birdie.

"**Oh no, you don't,**" Birdie shouted. "Don't you step one foot outside my door before you take back everything you've said to me," she demanded, trying to wrestle free.

"I'm not taking back anything," Moet told her. "First, you tried to say we shot you, and now you are trying to attack me. No way. I'm about to record this. The world is gonna know about my innocence." She told Birdie, pointing her phone at her.

"Give me that," Darius said, snatching her phone away from her and deleting what she had just recorded. Before he could say more, his phone was chiming from the multiple texting messages he was receiving. He looked at his phone to see frantic messages about him being on Facebook. He turns and glares at Moet.

"**What did you do?!**" He yelled at her.

"What do you mean? Besides prove our innocence, nothing." Darius looked on his Facebook page to find comments and wow emojis. "Delete this now!" He told her.

"But she said-"

"I don't care what she said; **delete it now!**" He demanded.

"**Thank you!**" Birdie shouted. "Having people all in my business, I don't think so. That's the last thing I need. I mind my own business, and don't be messing with nobody." Birdie proclaimed.

"Do tell," Darius said while smirking at Walter, who was side-eyeing his wife.

"That's right. I don't be in nobody's business, cause-"

"You don't mean nobody, but everybody's business." Walter corrected her.

"Walter, let me tell you something-" Birdie said, snapping.

Before Birdie could lay into her husband, Darius decided to interrupt her. "Um, Mr. Walter and Ms. Birdie, we're about to get out of here. Sorry to cause you any confusion. I'm glad to see that you're not hurt or anything like that, but we're leaving now." He said, backing out and closing the door behind him, smirking.

"Oooh Birdie, I can't wait to tell Alfreda all about this," Walt said, releasing her with tears rolling down his face from laughter.

"**You better not, Walter Abrams**! Don't you be telling my business, and I mean it." She was so embarrassed, especially after finding the puddle beneath her wasn't what she once thought.

"Yes I am, too. I am going to tell her how... how you were so caught up in somebody else's business... You accused them of shooting you, and... And the puddle you felt was not blood, but peeeee..." Walter laughed so hard that it made Birdie laugh. Woman you are crazy!

"That's not funny, Walt. It could've happened to anybody."

"Yeah, only nosey people, and you had the nerve to try to fight that young girl so she wouldn't tell it. Oooh, I can't wait."

"Hmph, I thought you didn't believe in gossip?" Birdie questioned him.

"Girl, this ain't no gossip. I saw you make a fool out of yourself with my own two eyes.

The way I see it, you owe me for my silence."

"Walter Abrams, you mean to tell me that you're going to actually stand there, and blackmail your wife?"

"Un-huh, if you have a right to peep on the neighbors, I have the right to collect payment for my silence, and I think I'll start by having breakfast in bed in the morning."

"It'll be a shame to have breakfast in bed to just eat cold soggy cereal." She warned him.

However, Walt didn't hold his wife to serving him breakfast in bed, but when he would catch Birdie being nosey or gossiping, he'd threaten to tell her secret. This also worked in Darius' favor, too. Birdie had to be nice to him also. "Doggone that Walt," she thought. This was the part of the agreement she didn't like. She'd rather serve him breakfast in bed. Birdie had even accepted an invitation to attend his upcoming wedding to Erica. To tell the truth, the only reason she really wanted to go was to see if anyone would show up and disrupt the ceremony.

Unfortunately for her, once Darius decided Erica was the one for him, there was no one else who could take her place. He eventually told Erica about his past, and as he once feared, she didn't want any parts of the drama, but something changed. She realized she couldn't hold him to his past. Everything that took place happened long before her. What truly mattered was what was happening now and in their future. If he was willing to change, and become a better man for himself first, and then her, why not allow him to prove it, and proved it he did. They had a beautiful outdoor ceremony a year later.

"It's been quiet around here lately, hasn't it Birdie?" Alfreda said as they sat on the porch.

"Yeah, too quiet, Freda."

"But you know how this neighborhood is. Give it a minute, and something crazy will happen soon."

"Chile, the last time we saw some good action was last year when Darius' parents came back from their trip." Birdie said, snickering.

"His mama cussed him up one way and down the other. I didn't even know she could talk like that."

"I felt sorry for him."

"Say what? You felt sorry for him?" Alfreda asked her in shock.

"Yeah, come to find out, all that mess was over nothing."

"Well, girl, you know how rumors get started, folks assume one thing, and tell another."

"That's a shame. For that reason, right there, we mind our own business."

"Yes we do, Birdie, like good watchful neighbors should."

"Hey Freda, look down the street at Pearl's old house. Isn't that one of her children?"

"It looks like her son, Edward."

"It sure is. I thought her children were going to sell her house and split the profits? They know they laid her away nicely. All those beautiful floral arrangements, family cars, and the programs were just nice. She must have had a good policy to afford all of that."

"She would've had to with all that stuff. Chile, you know these children don't believe in putting all that money in the ground. Honey, we better be glad they won't allow them to put us in a box somewhere. But I'm not sure, Birdie, about the house. I know it has been on the market for a while. I didn't think the listing price was too much for the neighborhood, did you?" Alfreda asked her.

"Not to me, but I did hear-"

"**Birdie!**" Walter called her name, and she knew what that meant. She had been caught gossiping.

"He's always in my business," She told Alfreda. "Folks can't even have a decent conversation in peace without somebody always eavesdropping."

"I guess our neighbors could say the same thing about you too, Birdie." Her husband replied.

"Well it's like I've always said, Birdie, it's better to be the one doing the talking, than the one being talked about."

"And for that reason, Alfreda, you're my friend," Birdie said as they laughed together.

"And for that same reason, Alfreda, I have something to tell you," Walter said, coming out on the porch.

"That's a doggone shame ain't nobody's business sacred anymore." Birdie said as she watched two former enemies, her husband, Walter, and dearest friend, Alfreda, share the greatest laugh at her expense in years. "Well, at least my being nosey was good for something." She told them and helped Walter, who was too tickled to tell the rest of the story.

Peepers: The Unsolicited Neighborhood Watch

Thank you for reading Peepers: The Unsolicited Neighborhood Watch. I pray this novella has made you laugh and reminisce about the people in your neighborhood. I thoroughly enjoyed

writing this story. Who hasn't had a nosey neighbor or two, right? I'd love to hear from you! Please share with me your thoughts and feedback about this story. Feel free to share the antics of your nosey neighbors, and what made you laugh the most. Please email me at ddmiles.relationshipreflections@gmail.com, or visit my website at https://relationshipreflections.org.

www.ingramcontent.com/pod-product-compliance
Lightning Source LLC
Chambersburg PA
CBHW030512130626
46549CB00007B/2949